WORKED IN THE ROUND

Love to cuddle up beneath a warm and cozy throw? Then choose your favorite pattern from this book, pick up your favorite colors of Red Heart® yarn, and get started. The projects in this book are fun to do because you are working in the round, and you can personalize them for any family member or friend by your color choices from the extensive Red Heart collection.

Super Saver®
Our best-selling yarn. Traditional hand, maximum wash performance, and no-dye-lot solids make it ideal for afghans, sweaters, accessories and more.

Super Saver® Chunky™
If you love Super Saver, you will surely adore this chunky weight version for quick and trendy accessories or home décor.

With Love®
Ultra soft, premium acrylic yarn perfect for throws, garments and accessories. Available in a beautiful range of mixable multis and no-dye-lot solids. Made for you, With Love, in the USA.

About Red Heart Yarns

Red Heart is one of the most trusted brands in yarn. For over 75 years more people have chosen to make American heirlooms using Red Heart yarn than any other yarn. Red Heart yarns stand for quality, largest color selection, fashion and above all else, crafted with love. Whatever your creativity calls for, you'll find it in the Red Heart family.

LEISURE ARTS, INC.
Maumelle, Arkansas

Weekend-Wonder
giant granny square throw

 **EASY**

Throw is 48" x 55" (122 cm x 140 cm).

SHOPPING LIST

Yarn (Bulky Weight)
RED HEART® Super Saver® Chunky™:
- ☐ 0312 Black **A** - 2 skeins
- ☐ 0334 Buff **B** - 2 skeins
- ☐ 0311 White **C** - 3 skeins

Crochet Hook
- ☐ 10 mm [US N-15]

Additional Supplies
- ☐ Yarn needle

GAUGE INFORMATION
Round 1 = 2½" x 3¾" long
(6.25 cm x 9.5 cm).
CHECK YOUR GAUGE. Use any
size hook to obtain the gauge.

▪Designed by Katherine Eng.

3

THROW

With **A**, ch 8.

Row 1: Slip st in 4th ch from hook (counts as ch-1 space), slip st in next 2 chs, ch 1, skip next ch, slip st in last ch – 2 ch-1 spaces.

Round 1 (Right side)**:** Ch 3 (counts as dc here and throughout), turn; work 2 dc in ch-1 space, ch 2, 3 dc in same space, ch 1, [(3 dc, ch 2) twice, 3 dc] in next ch-1 space, ch 1, 3 dc in first ch-1 space, ch 2; join with a slip st to top of beginning ch-3.

Fasten off.

Round 2: Join **B** with a slip st in any ch-1 space; ch 3, work 2 dc in same space, ch 1, [(3 dc, ch 2, 3 dc) in next ch-2 space, ch 1] twice, 3 dc in next ch-1 space, ch 1, [(3 dc, ch 2, 3 dc) in next ch-2 space, ch 1] twice; join with a slip st to top of beginning ch-3.

Round 3 (Wrong side)**:** Ch 3, turn; 2 dc in same ch-1 space, *ch 1, (3 dc, ch 2, 3 dc) in next corner ch-2 space, [ch 1, 3 dc in next ch-1 space] to next ch-2 space; repeat from * 2 times more, (3 dc, ch 2, 3 dc) in last corner ch-2 space, [ch 1, 3 dc in next ch-1 space] to beginning ch, ch 1; join with a slip st to top of beginning ch-3.

Fasten off.

Round 4: Join **C** with a slip st in any corner ch-2 space; ch 3, work 2 dc in same space, ch 2, 3 dc in same space, *[ch 1, 3 dc in next ch-1 space] across to next corner ch-2 space, ch 1, (3 dc, ch 2, 3 dc) in corner ch-2 space; repeat from * 2 times more, [ch 1, 3 dc in next ch-1 space] across to beginning ch, ch 1; join with a slip st to top of beginning ch-3.

Round 5: Ch 3, turn; 2 dc in same ch-1 space, *ch 1, [3 dc in next ch-1 space, ch 1] to next ch-2 space, (3 dc, ch 2, 3 dc) in corner ch-2 space; repeat from * 3 times more, ch 1; join with a slip st to top of beginning ch-3.

Round 6: Ch 3, turn; 2 dc in same ch-1 space, ch 1, *(3 dc, ch 2, 3 dc) in corner ch-2 space, ch 1, [3 dc in next ch-1 space, ch 1] to next ch-2 space; repeat from * 2 times more, (3 dc, ch 2, 3 dc) in corner ch-2 space, ch 1, [3 dc in next ch-1 space, ch 1] to beginning ch; join with a slip st to top of beginning ch-3.

Fasten off.

Rounds 7-8: With **A**, repeat Rounds 4-5.

Fasten off.

Round 9: With **B**, repeat Round 4.

Fasten off.

Round 10: With **C**, repeat Round 4.

Fasten off.

Round 11: With **A**, repeat Round 4.

Fasten off.

Rounds 12-13: With **B**, repeat Rounds 4-5.

Fasten off.

Rounds 14-16: With **C**, repeat Rounds 4-6.

Fasten off.

Rounds 17-18: With **A**, repeat Rounds 4-5.

Fasten off.

Round 19: With **B**, repeat Round 4.

Fasten off.

Round 20: With **C**, repeat Round 4.

Fasten off.

Round 21: With **A**, repeat Round 4.

Fasten off.

Rounds 22-23: With **B**, repeat Rounds 4-5.

Fasten off.

Rounds 24-26: With **C**, repeat Rounds 4-6.

Fasten off.

Rounds 27-28: With **A**, repeat Rounds 4-5.

Fasten off.

Round 29: With **B**, repeat Round 4.

Fasten off.

Round 30: With **C**, repeat Round 4.

Round 31: (Sc, ch 2, sc) in next dc, ch 1, skip next dc, *(sc, ch 2, sc) in next ch-2 space, [ch 1, (sc, ch 2, sc) in center dc of next dc-group, ch 1, slip st in next ch-1 space] across to next corner, ch 1, (sc, ch 2, sc) in center dc of next dc-group, ch 1; repeat from * 2 times more, (sc, ch 2, sc) in next ch-2 space, [ch 1, (sc, ch 2, sc) in center dc of next dc-group, ch 1, slip st in next ch-1 space] across to first sc; join with a slip st to first sc.

Fasten off.

Weave in ends.

Colorful twists & turns throw

(Shown on page 9)

◼◼◼▭ **INTERMEDIATE**

Throw measures 45" x 65" (114.5 cm x 165 cm)

SHOPPING LIST

Yarn (Medium Weight)
RED HEART® Super Saver®:
- ☐ 0505 Aruba Sea **A** - 2 skeins
- ☐ 0365 Coffee **B** - 2 skeins
- ☐ 0668 Honeydew **C** - 2 skeins
- ☐ 0336 Warm Brown **D** - 2 skeins
- ☐ 0512 Turqua **E** - 1 skein

Crochet Hook
- ☐ 6.5 mm [US K-10.5]

Additional Supplies
- ☐ Yarn needle
- ☐ Stitch markers

GAUGE INFORMATION

12 dc = 4" (10 cm); 6 rows = 4" (10 cm).
CHECK YOUR GAUGE. Use any size hook to obtain the gauge.

——**SPECIAL STITCHES**——

dc2tog (double crochet 2 together): [Yo, insert hook in next st, yo and pull up loop, yo and draw through 2 loops] 2 times, yo and draw through all 3 loops on hook.

Note: Throw begins in a circle, then is worked into a hexagon and finally ends up as a rectangle. Circle and Hexagon sections are worked in rounds. Rectangle sides are worked back and forth in rows. Colors can be carried along wrong side of work on narrower stripes.

THROW
Begin Circle

With **D**, ch 5; join with a slip st to form a ring.

Round 1 (Right side): Ch 5 (counts as tr and ch 1), [tr, ch 1] 11 times in ring; join with a slip st to 4th ch of beginning ch-5 – 12 tr. Fasten off.

Round 2: Join **C** with a slip st in any ch-1 space; ch 3 (counts as dc here and throughout), dc in same space, [ch 1, 2 dc in next ch-1 space] around, ch 1; join with a slip st to top of beginning ch-3 – 24 dc. Fasten off.

Round 3: Join **D** with a slip st in any ch-1 space; ch 3, dc in same space, dc in next dc, *ch 1, skip next dc, 2 dc in next ch-1 space, dc in next dc; repeat from * 10 times more, ch 1; join with a slip st to top of beginning ch-3 – 36 dc. Fasten off.

Round 4: Join **B** with a slip st in any ch-1 space; ch 3, dc in same space, *dc in next 2 dc, ch 1, skip next dc, 2 dc in next ch-1 space; repeat from * around to last 3 dc, dc in next 2 dc, ch 1, skip last dc; join with a slip st to top of beginning ch-3 – 48 dc.

Round 5: Ch 3, dc in last ch-1 space of previous row, *dc in next 3 dc, ch 1, skip next dc, 2 dc in next ch-1 space; repeat from * around to last 4 dc, dc in next 3 dc, ch 1, skip last dc; join with a slip st to top of beginning ch-3 – 60 dc.

Designed by Ann Regis.

Round 6: Ch 3, dc in same ch-1 space, *dc in each dc across to last dc before ch-1 space, ch 1, skip next dc, 2 dc in next ch-1 space; repeat from * around, dc in each dc across to last dc, ch 1, skip last dc; join with a slip st to top of beginning ch-3 –72 dc; 12 dc increased.
Fasten off.

Rounds 7 and 13: Join **D** with a slip st in any ch-1 space; repeat Round 6.
Fasten off.

Rounds 8, 10 and 12: Join **C** with a slip st in any ch-1 space; repeat Round 6.
Fasten off.

Rounds 9 and 11: Join **E** with a slip st in any ch-1 space and working in hdc, repeat Round 6.
Fasten off.

Rounds 14 and 15: Join **B** with a slip st in any ch-1 space; repeat Round 6 but do not fasten off – 180 dc; 15 dc between ch-1 spaces on last round.

Begin Hexagon

Round 16: Ch 3, *dc in each dc to next ch-1 space, skip ch-1 space, dc in each dc to next ch-1 space, (dc, ch 1, dc) in ch-1 space for first hexagon point; repeat from * 4 times more, dc in each dc to next ch-1 space, skip ch-1 space, dc in each dc to last ch-1 space, dc in ch-1 space, ch 1; join with a slip st to top of beginning ch-3 for 6th hexagon point.

Round 17: Ch 3, *dc in next 15 dc, dc2tog, dc in each dc to next ch-1 space, (dc, ch 1, dc) in ch-1 space; repeat from * 4 times more, dc in next 15 dc, dc2tog, dc in each dc to last ch-1 space, dc in last ch-1 space, ch 1; join with a slip st to top of beginning ch-3.

Round 18: Ch 3, *dc in next 16 dc, dc2tog, dc in each dc to next ch-1 space, (dc, ch 1, dc) in ch-1 space; repeat from * 4 times more, dc in next 16 dc, dc2tog, dc in each dc to last ch-1 space, dc in ch-1 space, ch 1; join with a slip st to top of beginning ch-3.
Fasten off.

Round 19: Join **A** with a slip st in any ch-1 space; ch 3, dc in each dc to next ch-1 space, (dc, ch 1, dc) in ch-1 space; repeat from *

4 times more, dc in each dc to last ch-1 space, dc in last ch-1 space, ch 1; join with a slip st to top of beginning ch-3.

Rounds 20-21: Ch 3, working in back loops only *(Fig. 4, page 47)*, dc in each dc to next ch-1 space, (dc, ch 1, dc) in ch-1 space; repeat from * 4 times more, dc in each dc to last ch-1 space, dc in ch-1 space, ch 1; join with a slip st to top of beginning ch-3. Fasten off.

Rounds 22 and 26: Join **D** with a slip st in any ch-1 space and working in hdc, repeat Round 20. Fasten off.

Rounds 23 and 25: Join **C** with a slip st in any ch-1 space and working in hdc, repeat Round 20. Fasten off.

Round 24: Join **E** with a slip st in any ch-1 space and working in dc, repeat Round 20. Fasten off.

Rounds 27-29: Join **A** with a slip st in any ch-1 space and working in dc, repeat Round 20. Fasten off.

Rounds 30-31: Join **B** with a slip st in any ch-1 space and working in dc, repeat Round 20. Fasten off.

Begin Rectangle
FIRST END
Row 1: With right side facing, join **B** with a slip st in any ch-1 space for Point 1; ch 3, working in back loops only, dc in first dc, dc2tog, dc in each dc to 6 sts before next ch-1 space (Point 2), hdc in next 3 dc, mark first hdc worked, sc in next 3 dc, skip ch-1 space, sc in next 3 dc, hdc in next 3 dc, mark last hdc worked, dc across to 3 dc before next ch-1 space, dc2tog, dc in last dc, dc in ch-1 space (Point 3).

Diagram

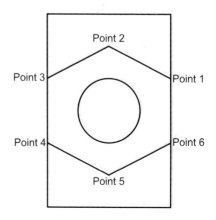

Row 2: Ch 3, turn; working through both loops, dc in next dc, dc2tog, dc to 3 dc before marked hdc, hdc in next 3 dc, mark first hdc worked, sc in each st to next marked st, hdc in next 3 dc, mark last hdc worked, dc across to last 4 sts, dc2tog, dc in last 2 sts.

Row 3: Working through back loops only, repeat Row 2.

Row 4: Working through both loops, repeat Row 2.
Fasten off.

Rows 5-8: With **A**, repeat Rows 3-4 twice.
Fasten off.

Rows 9-11: With **D**, repeat Rows 3-4 once, then repeat Row 3 once more.

Row 12: Ch 2, turn; sc in each st across to first marker, hdc in next 3 sts, dc across to 3 sts before next marker, hdc in next 3 sts, sc across.
Fasten off.

SECOND END
Row 1: With right side facing, join **B** with a slip st at Point 4 and work - for First End.

SIDE EDGES
With right side facing and matching colors, work 1 row of sc evenly spaced along each side edge.
Fasten off.

Finishing
Matching colors, work sc evenly spaced along each edge of Throw.

BORDER
Round 1: With right side facing, join **D** with a slip st to any corner st; ch 3, dc in same st, [dc in each st to opposite corner st, (2 dc, ch 3, 2 dc) in st just after corner] 3 times, dc in each st to first corner, 2 dc in last st, ch 3; join with a slip st to top of beginning ch-3.
Fasten off.

Round 2: With right side facing, join **C** with a slip st to any ch-3 space; ch 2, hdc in same space, hdc in each st around, working (2 hdc, ch 2, 2 hdc) in each corner ch-3 space, 2 hdc in first corner, ch 2; join with a slip st to top of beginning ch-2.
Fasten off.

,urearts.com

Rounds 3 and 5: Join **E** with a slip st in any corner ch-space; ch 3, dc in each dc around, working (dc, ch 2, dc) in each corner ch-space, dc in first corner, ch 2; join with a slip st to top of beginning ch-3. Fasten off.

Rounds 4 and 6: Join **C** with a slip st in any corner ch-space; ch 2, hdc in each dc around, working (hdc, ch 2, hdc) in each corner ch-space, hdc in first corner, ch 2; join with a slip st to top of beginning ch-2. Fasten off.

Round 7: Join **D** with a slip st in any corner ch-space; ch 3, dc in each dc around, working (dc, ch 2, dc) in each corner ch-space, dc in first corner, ch 2; join with a slip st to top of beginning ch-3. Fasten off.

Round 8: Join **A** with a slip st in any corner ch-space; ch 3, dc in each dc around, working (dc, ch 2, dc) in each corner ch-space, dc in first corner, ch 2; join with a slip st to top of beginning ch-3. Fasten off.

CORDED EDGE

Round 1: With right side facing, join **B** with a slip st in any dc; ch 1, sc in same st, [ch 3, skip next dc, sc in next dc] around, working in ch-2 space in corners if necessary; join with a slip st to first sc. Fasten off.

Round 2: With right side facing, join **A** with a slip st in any ch-3 space; *ch 4, remove hook from st (open st), insert hook from front to back through next ch-3 space and into open st and pull through ch-3 space to front of work; repeat from * around; join with a slip st to first slip st. Fasten off.

Weave in ends.

7-Point Star throw

■■■□ INTERMEDIATE

Throw measures 62" (157.5 cm) in diameter.

SHOPPING LIST

Yarn (Medium Weight) 🧶 **4**
RED HEART® Super Saver®:
- ☐ 0946 Peruvian Print **A** - 4 skeins
- ☐ 0656 Real Teal **B** - 2 skeins
- ☐ 0624 Tea Leaf **C** - 1 skein
- ☐ 0256 Carrot **D** - 1 skein

Crochet Hooks
- ☐ 6 mm [US J-10] **and**
- ☐ 6.5 mm [US K-10.5]

Additional Supplies
- ☐ Yarn needle
- ☐ Tapestry needle

GAUGE INFORMATION

12 sts = 4" (10 cm); 7 rows = 4" (10 cm) in dc with larger hook. **CHECK YOUR GAUGE. Use any size hook to obtain the gauge.**

——SPECIAL STITCHES——

inc (increase): 2 Dc in next dc.
dec3 (decrease): Yo, insert hook in next dc, yo and pull up a loop, yo and draw through 2 loops, skip next dc, yo, insert hook in next dc, yo and pull up a loop, yo and draw through 2 loops, yo and draw through all 3 loops on hook.

Designed by Ann Regis.

Note: Join and cut colors as required, always joining new color with a slip st in a ch-2 space. When possible, carry yarns loosely along wrong side of work, twisting every other row to avoid long strands.

THROW

With larger hook and **C**, ch 5; join with a slip st to form a ring.

Round 1 (Right side): Ch 3 (counts as a dc), 15 dc in ring; join with a slip st to top of beginning ch-3 – 16 dc.

Round 2: Ch 3, dc in same st as joining, inc in each dc around; join with a slip st to top of beginning ch-3 – 32 dc.

Round 3: Ch 3, dc in same st as joining, [inc, dc in next dc] 15 times, inc in last dc; join with a slip st to top of beginning ch-3 – 49 dc.

Round 4: Join **A** with a slip st in same st as joining; ch 3, dc in next dc, [inc, dc in next 3 dc, inc, dc in next 2 dc] 6 times, inc, dc in next 3 dc, inc; join with a slip st to top of beginning ch-3 – 63 dc.

Round 5: With **C**, ch 3, dc in next 2 dc, dec3, dc in next 3 dc, [ch 2, dc in next 3 dc, dec3, dc in next 3 dc] 6 times, ch 2; join with a slip st to top of beginning ch-3 – 7 ch-2 spaces and 49 dc (7 dc between ch-2 spaces).

Round 6: Join **A** with a slip st in any ch-2 space; ch 3, *[inc] twice, dec3 (skipping dec3 of previous **round**), [inc] twice **, (dc, ch 2, dc) in ch-2 space; repeat from * to last space, end at **, dc in last space, *ch 1, hdc in top of ch-3 to join and form last space* – **row ended**. – 7 ch-2 spaces and 77 dc (11 dc between ch-2 sps).

Note: Work the first inc of each following round in the top of the beginning ch-3 of the previous round (in the same place as the joining hdc).

Round 7: Ch 3, *[inc] twice, dc in next 2 dc, dec3 (skipping dec3 of previous **round**), dc in next 2 dc, [inc] twice **, (dc, ch 2, dc) all in ch-2 space; repeat from * to last space, end at **, dc in last space, end row (see italicized text at end of Round 6) – 7 ch-2 spaces and 15 dc between ch-2 sps.

Round 8: Ch 3, *[inc] twice, dc in next 4 dc, dec3, dc in next 4 dc, [inc] twice **, (dc, ch 2, dc) all in ch-2 space; repeat from * to last space, end at **, dc in last space, end row – 7 ch-2 spaces and 19 dc between ch-2 sps.

Round 9: With **C**, ch 3, *inc, dc in next 7 dc, dec3, dc in next 7 dc, inc **, (dc, ch 2, dc) all in ch-2 space; repeat from * to last space, end at **, dc in last space, end row – 7 ch-2 spaces and 21 dc between ch-2 spaces.

Round 10: With **A**, ch 3, *inc, dc in next 8 dc, dec3, dc in next 8 dc, inc **, (dc, ch 2, dc) all in ch-2 space; repeat from * to last space, end at **, dc in last space, end row – 7 ch-2 spaces and 23 dc between ch-2 spaces.

Round 11: With **D**, ch 3, *inc, dc in next 9 dc, dec3, dc in next 9 dc, inc, (dc, ch 2, dc) all in ch-2 space; repeat from * to last space, end at **, dc in last space, end row – 7 ch-2 spaces and 25 dc between ch-2 spaces.

Repeat **Round 11** (working 1 more dc before and after center dec3) in colors as follows:

Rounds 12-13: **A** (working 1 dc in next 10 dc on **Round 12**, then in next 11 dc on **Round 13**).

Round 14: **D**.

Rounds 15-16: **A**.

Round 17: **D**.

Round 18: **A**.

Round 19: **C**.

Round 20: **A**.

Round 21: **C**.

Round 22: **A**.

Round 23: **C**.

Round 24: **A**.

Round 25: **C**. There will be 26 dc before and after center dec3. Cut yarn.

Round 26: Join **A** with a slip st in any ch-2 space; ch 3, *[inc, dc in next 6 dc, dec3, dc in next 6 dc, inc, (dc, ch 2, dc) all in next dc] twice, inc, dc in next 6 dc, dec3, dc in next 6 dc, inc **, (dc, ch 2, dc) all in next ch-2 space; repeat from * to last space, end at **, dc in last space, end row – two ch-2 spaces have been added between each of the original ch-2 spaces.

Round 27: Ch 3, *inc, dc in next 7 dc, dec3, dc in next 7 dc, inc **, (dc, ch 2, dc) all in next ch-2 space; repeat from * to last space, end at **, dc in last space, end row.

Round 28: With **C**, ch 3, *inc, dc in next 8 dc, dec3, dc in next 8 dc, inc **, (dc, ch 2, dc) all in next ch-2 space; repeat from * to last space, end at **, dc in last space, end row.

Repeat **Round 28** in colors as follows, working 1 more dc before and after dec3:

Rounds 29-30: A.

Round 31: D.

Round 32: A.

Round 33: D.

Round 34: A.

Rounds 35-38: B.
Fasten off.

Weave in ends.

Finishing

With right side facing and smaller hook, join **C** with a slip st in any ch-2 space; ch 1, slip st evenly (being careful not to pull too tightly) around entire piece, working into each dc and ch-2 space; join with a slip st to first st. Fasten off.

With tapestry needle and **D**, work a running st along edge as follows: *bring yarn up through a st from wrong side to right side, then down through the next st, skip next 2 sts; repeat from * around. Fasten off.

Weave in ends.

Octagons & Squares
throw

◼◼◻◻ **EASY**

Throw measures 47" x 58" (119.5 cm x 147.5 cm).

SHOPPING LIST

Yarn (Medium Weight) **4** MEDIUM

RED HEART® With Love®:

☐ 1538 Lilac **A** - 1 skein
☐ 1308 Tan **B** - 2 skeins
☐ 1601 Lettuce **C** - 2 skeins
☐ 1701 Hot Pink **D** - 2 skeins

Crochet Hook

☐ 6 mm [US J-10]

Additional Supplies

☐ Yarn needle

GAUGE INFORMATION

11 dc = 4" (10 cm); Motif #2 = 5½" (14 cm) square.

CHECK YOUR GAUGE. Use any size hook to obtain the gauge.

—— SPECIAL STITCHES ——

Beginning bobble: Ch 3 (counts as dc), work 2 dc in indicated st leaving the last loop of each st on the hook, yo and draw through all 3 loops on hook.

Bobble: Work 3 dc in indicated st leaving the last loop of each st on the hook, yo and draw through all 4 loops on hook.

THROW
Motif 1

(Make 10 with C, 10 with D)
With **A**, ch 5; join with a slip st to form a ring.

Round 1: Beginning bobble in ring, [ch 2, bobble in ring] 7 times, ch 2; join with a slip st to top of beginning bobble – 8 bobbles. Fasten off **A**.

Round 2: Join **B** with a slip st in any ch-2 space; (beginning bobble, ch 2, bobble) in same space, *(ch 2, bobble, ch 2, bobble) in next ch-2 space; repeat from * around, ch 2; join with a slip st to top of beginning bobble – 16 bobbles. Fasten off **B**.

Round 3: Join **C** or **D** with a slip st in ch-2 space between beginning bobble and next bobble; (ch 3, dc) in same space, [dc in next ch-2 space, (2 dc, ch 2, 2 dc) in next ch-2 space] 7 times, dc in next ch-2 space, 2 dc in first ch-2 space; join with hdc to top of beginning ch-3 – 8 corner ch-2 spaces; 40 dc (5 dc each side).

Round 4: Ch 3, [dc in next 5 dc, (dc, ch 1, dc) in corner ch-2 space] 7 times, dc in next 5 dc, dc in first space; join with hdc to top of beginning ch-3 – 56 dc (7 dc each side).

Round 5: Ch 3, [dc in next 7 dc, (dc, ch 1, dc) in corner ch-1 space] 7 times, dc in next 7 dc, dc in first space; join with hdc to top of beginning ch-3 – 72 dc (9 dc each side).

Round 6: Ch 3, [dc in next 9 dc, (dc, ch 1, dc) in corner ch-1 space] 7 times, dc in next 9 dc, dc in first space; join with hdc to top of beginning ch-3 – 88 dc (11 dc each side).

Round 7: Ch 3, [dc in next 11 dc, (dc, ch 1, dc) in corner ch-1 space] 7 times, dc in next 11 dc, dc in first space; join with hdc to top of beginning ch-3 – 104 dc (13 dc each side). Fasten off.

Round 8: Join **B** with a slip st in any ch-1 space; ch 1, sc in same space, [sc in next 13 dc, (sc, ch 1, sc) in corner ch-1 space] 7 times, sc in next 13 dc, sc in first ch-1 space; join with hdc to first sc – 120 dc (15 sc each side). Fasten off.

Weave in ends.

Motif 2
(Make 6 with C, 6 with D)
With **C** or **D**, ch 5; join with a slip st to form a ring.

Round 1: Beginning bobble in ring, [ch 2, bobble in ring] 7 times, ch 2; join with a slip st to top of beginning bobble – 8 bobbles. Fasten off.

Round 2: Join **A** with a slip st in any ch-2 space; [beginning bobble, ch 3, bobble] in same space for corner, *ch 2, [bobble, ch 2, bobble] in next ch-2 space, ch 2**, [bobble, ch 3, bobble] in next ch-2 space for corner; repeat from * 3 times, ending last repeat at **; join with a slip st to top of beginning bobble – 16 bobbles; 4 corners. Fasten off.

Round 3: Join **B** with a slip st in any corner ch-3 space; ch 3 (counts as dc), 2 dc in same space, *2 dc in next ch-2 space, 3 dc in next ch-2 space, 2 dc in next ch-2 space**, [3 dc, ch 2, 3 dc] in next ch-3 space; repeat from * 3 times, ending last repeat at **, 3 dc in first corner ch-3 space, ch 1; join with hdc to top of beginning ch-3 – 52 dc (13 dc each side).

Round 4: Ch 1, sc in same space, [sc in next 13 dc, (sc, ch 1, sc) in corner ch-2 space] 3 times, sc in next 13 dc, sc in first space; join with hdc to first sc – 60 sc (15 sc each side). Fasten off.

Weave in ends.

Finishing

With **B**, slip st octagons and squares together, using Assembly Diagram as a guide for placement.

Weave in ends.

Assembly Diagram

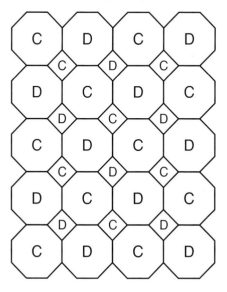

Spectrum throw

■■■■▭ INTERMEDIATE

Throw measures 49" x 57" (124.5 cm x 145 cm).

SHOPPING LIST

Yarn (Medium Weight) **4 MEDIUM**
RED HEART® Super Saver®:
- ☐ 0365 Coffee **MC** - 3 skeins
- ☐ 0358 Lavender **A** - 1 skein
- ☐ 0668 Honeydew **B** - 1 skein
- ☐ 0360 Café Latte **C** - 1 skein
- ☐ 0313 Aran **D** - 1 skein
- ☐ 0505 Aruba Sea **E** - 1 skein
- ☐ 0334 Buff **F** - 1 skein

Crochet Hook
- ☐ 6 mm [US I-9]

Additional Supplies
- ☐ Yarn needle

GAUGE INFORMATION
Square = 6" x 6" (15.25 cm). **CHECK YOUR GAUGE.**
Use any size hook to obtain the gauge.

── SPECIAL STITCHES ──

FPtr (Front Post treble crochet):
Yo (twice), insert hook from the front side of the work to back and to front again around the post of the indicated st on a previous row *(Fig. 5, page 47)*, yo and pull up a loop (4 loops on hook), yo and draw through 2 loops (3 loops on hook), yo and draw through 2 loops (2 loops on hook), yo and draw through 2 loops (1 loop on hook).

sc3tog (single crochet 3 together): [Draw up a loop in next st] 3 times, yo and draw through all 4 loops on hook.

──────────────────

THROW

Color Sequences
SQUARES 1, 2, 3, 6, 9
(make 8 each)
Work 1 round each in the following color sequences:
Square 1: A, B, C, D, MC
Square 2: E, D, F, B, MC
Square 3: F, C, A, B, MC
Square 6: C, A, B, F, MC
Square 9: A, E, B, D, MC

SQUARES 4, 5, 7, 8 (make 7 each)
Work 1 round each in the following color sequences:
Square 4: C, F, D, E, MC
Square 5: B, F, E, A, MC
Square 7: D, E, F, C, MC
Square 8: B, A, D, E, MC

Square

With first color, ch 6; join with a slip st to form a ring.

Round 1: Ch 4, 3 tr in ring, [ch 3, 4 tr] 3 times in ring, ch 3; join with a slip st to top of beginning ch-4. Fasten off.

Round 2: With right side facing, join 2nd color with a slip st in any ch-3 space; ch 3, (2 dc, ch 2, 3 dc) in same space, sc in next 4 sts, *(3 dc, ch 2, 3 dc) in next ch-3 space, sc in next 4 sts; repeat from * twice; join with a slip st to top of beginning ch-3. Fasten off.

Round 3: With right side facing, join 3rd color with a slip st in any ch-2 space; ch 1, *(2 sc, ch 2, 2 sc) in ch-2 space, sc in next 2 dc, hdc in next dc, dc in next 4 sc, hdc in next dc, sc in next 2 dc; repeat from * around; join with a slip st to first sc. Fasten off.

Round 4: With right side facing, join 4th color with a slip st in any corner ch-2 space; ch 1, *(sc, ch 2, sc) in ch-2 space, sc in each st across to next corner space; repeat from * around; join with a slip st to first sc. Fasten off.

Round 5: With right side facing, join **MC** with a slip st in sc before any corner ch-2 space; ch 2, *(hdc, ch 2, hdc) in next ch-2 space, hdc in next 7 sc, [FPtr in next corresponding dc 2 rows below] twice, skip next 2 sc of Round 4 behind 2 FPtr**, hdc in next 7 sc; repeat from * around, ending last repeat at **, hdc in last 6 sc; join with a slip st to top of beginning ch-2. Fasten off.

Weave in ends.

Finishing
Sew squares together through back loops ONLY *(Fig. 4, page 47)* following Assembly Diagram.

Border
Round 1: With right side facing, join **MC** with a slip st in any corner ch-2 space; ch 1, sc evenly around, working 3 sc in each outside corner ch-2 space, and sc3tog at each inside corner to keep work laying flat; join with a slip st to first sc.

Round 2: Ch 1, sc evenly around, working 3 sc in each outside corner sc, and sc3tog at each inside corner to keep work laying flat; join with a slip st to first sc. Fasten off.

Weave in ends.

Assembly Diagram

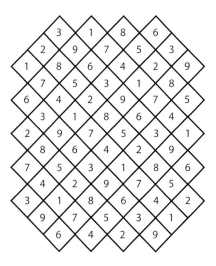

Medallion
circular afghan

■■■▭ **INTERMEDIATE**

Throw measures 62" (157.5 cm) in diameter.

SHOPPING LIST

Yarn (Medium Weight) 🧶**4** MEDIUM
RED HEART® Super Saver®:
☐ 0995 Ocean - 13 skeins

Crochet Hook
☐ 6.5 mm [US K-10.5]

Additional Supplies
☐ Split ring stitch markers - 56
☐ Yarn needle

GAUGE INFORMATION
First 3 rounds = 5" (12.75 cm) in diameter.
CHECK YOUR GAUGE. Use any size hook to obtain the gauge.

Designed by Ellen Gormley.

— SPECIAL STITCHES —

beg cl (beginning cluster):
Ch 2, [yo, insert hook in st or sp indicated, yo and draw up a loop, yo and draw through 2 loops on hook] twice, yo and draw through all 3 loops on hook.

cl (cluster): [Yo, insert hook in st or space indicated, yo and draw up a loop, yo and draw through 2 loops on hook] 3 times, yo and draw through all 4 loops on hook.

Notes: All rounds are worked on right side. Medallions are joined in a counterclockwise direction to last round worked on center.

AFGHAN
Center

Ch 4; join with a slip st to form a ring.

Round 1 (Right side): Ch 3 (counts as first dc now and throughout), 15 dc in ring; join with a slip st to top of beginning ch-3 – 16 dc.

Round 2: Ch 5 (counts as first dc and ch-2 space now and throughout); *skip next dc, dc in next dc, ch 2; repeat from * 6 times more; join with a slip st to 3rd ch of beginning ch-5 – 8 dc.

Round 3: Slip st in next ch-2 space, work beg cl in same ch-2 space as joining, ch 5, *(cl, ch 5) in next ch-2 space; repeat from * 6 times more; join with a slip st to top of beg cl – 8 cl.

Round 4: Slip st in back loop of next ch *(Fig. 1)*, ch 4 (counts as first tr), tr in back loop of same st, [2 tr in back loop of next ch] 3 times, ch 1, *skip next ch and cl, [2 tr in back loop of next ch] 4 times, ch 1; repeat from * 6 times more; join with a slip st to top of beginning ch-4 – 64 tr.

Fig. 1

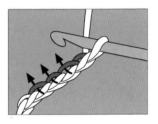

Round 5: Ch 5 (counts as first dc and ch-2 space), skip next tr, [dc in next tr, ch 2, skip next tr] 3 times, skip next ch-1 sp, *[dc in next tr, ch 2, skip next tr] 4 times, skip next ch-1 sp; repeat from * 6 times more; join with a slip st to 3rd ch of beginning ch-5 – 32 dc.

Round 6: Slip st in next ch-2 space, work beg cl in same ch-2 space as joining, ch 2, *cl in next ch-2 space, ch 2; repeat from * around; join with a slip st to top of beg cl – 32 cl.

Round 7: Ch 3, dc in next ch, ch 1, *dc in next 3 sts (ch, cl and ch), ch 1; repeat from * around to last ch, dc in last ch; join with a slip st to top of beginning ch-3 – 96 dc.

Round 8: Ch 4 (counts as first tr), tr in each dc and ch-1 space around; join with a slip st to top of beginning ch-4 – 128 tr.

Fasten off.

First Medallion Section

Double-check st count on Round 8 before beginning medallions. Place marker in any st on Round 8; *skip next 7 sts, place marker in next st on Round 8; repeat from * around for a total of 16 markers placed.

FIRST MEDALLION

Ch 4; join with a slip st to form a ring.

Round 1 (Right side): Ch 3 (counts as first dc now and throughout), 15 dc in ring; join with a slip st to top of beginning ch-3 – 16 dc.

Round 2: Ch 3 (counts as first dc), slip st in any marked st on last round of center, dc in next dc on Round 1 of medallion, slip st in 2nd st before same marked st on last round of center, dc in next dc on Round 1 of medallion, slip st in 4th st before same marked st on last round of center, dc in next dc on Round 1 of medallion, [ch 1, dc in next st on Round 1 of medallion] 12 times, ch 1; join with a slip st to top of beginning ch-3 – 16 dc.

Fasten off.

SECOND MEDALLION
Ch 4; join with a slip st to form a ring.

Round 1 (Right side): Work same as Round 1 on first medallion.

Round 2: Ch 3 (counts as first dc), slip st in next marked st on last round of center (counterclockwise from last marked st), dc in next dc on Round 1 of medallion, slip st in 2nd st before same marked st on last round of center, dc in next dc on Round 1 of medallion, slip st in 4th st before same marked st on last round of center, dc in next dc on Round 1 of medallion, [ch 1, dc in next dc on Round 1 of medallion] 2 times, slip st in ch-1 space between 14th and 15th dc on previous medallion, dc in next dc on Round 1 of current medallion, [ch 1, dc in next dc on current medallion] 9 times, ch 1; join with a slip st to top of beginning ch-3 – 16 dc.

Fasten off.

Repeat 2nd medallion the number of times necessary around last round of center until one unworked st marker remains in last round.

LAST MEDALLION

Ch 4; join with a slip st to form a ring.

Round 1 (Right side): Work same as Round 1 on first medallion.

Round 2: Ch 3 (counts as first dc), slip st in last marked st on last round of center, dc in next dc on Round 1 of medallion, slip st in 2nd st before same marked st on last round of center, dc in next dc on Round 1 of medallion, slip st in 4th st before same marked st on last round of center, dc in next dc on Round 1 of medallion, [ch 1, dc in next dc on Round 1 of medallion] 2 times, slip st in ch-1 space between 14th and 15th dc on previous medallion, dc in next dc on Round 1 of current medallion, [ch 1, dc in next dc on current medallion] 7 times, slip st in ch-1 space between 6th and 7th dc on first medallion, [dc in next dc on current medallion, ch 1] 2 times; join with a slip st to top of beginning ch-3 – 16 dc.

Fasten off.

Remove all markers.

Center Continued

Round 9: Sc in 9th dc on any medallion, [sc in next ch-1 space, sc in next dc] 3 times, ch 5, *sc in 9th dc on next medallion, [sc in next ch-1 space, sc in next dc] 3 times, ch 5; repeat from * around; join with a slip st to first sc – 112 sc.

Fasten off.

Round 10: Join yarn with a slip st in next ch-5 space; ch 1, 3 sc in same ch-5 space, tr around joining slip st between 2 medallions directly below, 3 sc in same ch-5 space, sc in next 7 sc, *3 sc in next ch-5 space, tr around joining slip st between 2 medallions directly below, 3 sc in same ch-5 space, sc in next 7 sc; repeat from * around; join with a slip st to first sc – 208 sc and 16 tr.

Round 11: Slip st across to next tr, ch 4 (counts as first dc and ch-1 space), skip next st, *dc in next st, ch 1, skip next st; repeat from * around; join with a slip st to 3rd ch of beginning ch-4 – 112 dc.

Round 12: Slip st in next ch-1 space, work beg cl in same ch-1 space, ch 1, *cl in next ch-1 space, ch 1; repeat from * around; join with a slip st to top of beg cl – 112 cl.

Round 13: Slip st in next ch, ch 3, dc in each cl and ch around; join with a slip st to top of beginning ch-3 – 224 dc.

Round 14: Ch 4 (counts as first tr), tr in each st around; join with a slip st to top of beginning ch-4 – 224 tr.

Fasten off.

Second Medallion Section

Double-check st count on Round 14 before beginning medallions. Place marker in any st on Round 14; *skip next 7 sts, place marker in next st on Round 14; repeat from * around for a total of 28 markers placed.

Work 28 medallions same as First Medallion Section.

Remove all markers.

Center Continued

Round 15: Repeat Round 9 – 196 sc.

Round 16: Repeat Round 10 – 364 sc and 28 tr.

Round 17: Slip st across to next tr, ch 5 (counts as first dc and ch-2 space), skip next 3 sts, *dc in next st, ch 2, skip next 3 sts; repeat from * around; join with a slip st to 3rd ch of beginning ch-5 – 98 dc.

Round 18: Slip st in next ch-2 space, work beg cl in same ch-2 space, ch 3, *cl in next ch-2 space, ch 3; repeat from * around; join with a slip st in top of beg cl – 98 cl.

Round 19: Repeat Round 13 – 392 dc.

Round 20: Repeat Round 14 – 392 tr.

Fasten off.

Third Medallion Section

Double-check st count on Round 20 before beginning medallions. Place marker in any st on Round 20; *skip next 7 sts, place marker in next st on Round 20; repeat from * around for a total of 49 markers placed.

Work 49 medallions same as First Medallion Section.

Remove all markers.

Center Continued

Round 21: Repeat Round 9 – 343 sc.

Round 22: Repeat Round 10 – 637 sc and 49 tr.

Round 23: Repeat Round 11 – 343 dc.

Round 24: Slip st in next ch-1 space, work beg cl in same ch-1 space, ch 2, [skip next ch-1 space, cl in next ch-1 space, ch 2] 41 times, skip next ch-1 space, cl in next ch-1 space, ch 1, *[skip next ch-1 space, cl in next ch-1 space, ch 2] 42 times, skip next ch-1 space, cl in next ch-1 space, ch 1; repeat from * 2 times more; join with a slip st to top of beg cl – 172 cl and 340 chs.

Note: There is no ch-1 space skipped between last and first cl on Round 24.

Round 25: Repeat Round 13 – 512 dc.

Round 26: Ch 4 (counts as first tr), tr in next 6 sts, skip next st, *tr in next 7 sts, skip next st; repeat from * around; join with a slip st to top of beginning ch-4 – 448 tr.

Fasten off.

Fourth Medallion Section

Double-check st count on Round 26 before beginning medallions. Place marker in any st on Round 26; *skip next 7 sts, place marker in next st on Round 26; repeat from * around for a total of 56 markers placed.

Work 56 medallions same as First Medallion Section.

Remove all markers.

Center Continued

Round 27: Repeat Round 9 – 392 sc.

Round 28: Repeat Round 10 – 728 sc and 56 tr.

Round 29: Slip st across to next tr, ch 4 (counts as first dc and ch-1 space), *skip next 2 sts, dc in next st, ch 1; repeat from * around, skip last 3 sts; join with a slip st to 3rd ch of beginning ch-4 – 261 dc.

Round 30: Repeat Round 12 – 261 cl.

Round 31: Repeat Round 13 – 522 dc.

Round 32: Repeat Round 14 – 522 tr.

Round 33: Sc in first tr, cl in each of next 2 sts, sc in next st, [sc in next st, cl in each of next 2 sts, sc in next st] 64 times, skip next st, [sc in next st, cl in each of next 2 sts, sc in next st] 65 times, skip next st; join with a slip st to first sc – 260 cl and 260 sc.

Fasten off.

Weave in ends.

Diagrams

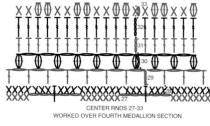

CENTER RNDS 27-33
WORKED OVER FOURTH MEDALLION SECTION

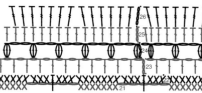

CENTER RNDS 21-26
WORKED OVER THIRD MEDALLION SECTION

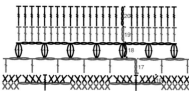

CENTER RNDS 17-20
WORKED OVER SECOND MEDALLION SECTION

Catherine's Wheel
throw

(Shown on page 39)

◖■■■▭ **INTERMEDIATE**

Throw measures 50" x 50" (127 cm x 127 cm).

SHOPPING LIST

Yarn (Medium Weight)
RED HEART® Super Saver®:
- ☐ 0964 Primary **A** - 3 skeins
- ☐ 0320 Cornmeal **B** - 3 skeins
- ☐ 0624 Tea Leaf **C** - 2 skeins
- ☐ 0378 Claret **D** - 2 skeins

Crochet Hook
- ☐ 5.5 mm [US I-9]

Additional Supplies
- ☐ Yarn needle

GAUGE INFORMATION

12 tr = 4" (10 cm); 4 rows = 4" (10 cm).
CHECK YOUR GAUGE. Use any size hook to obtain the gauge.

── SPECIAL STITCHES ──

On all back post (**BP**) sts, make the type of st indicated by inserting hook from the back, around in front of the post and out again to the back *(Fig. 2)*.

Fig. 2

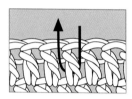

Partial tr (partial treble crochet): Yo twice, insert hook in st or space and pull up a loop, [yo and pull through 2 loops on hook] 2 times.
Partial BPtr (partial Back Post treble crochet): Yo twice, insert hook from the back, around in front of the post and out again to the back again around the post of st indicated, yo and pull up a loop, [yo and pull through 2 loops on hook] 2 times.
Reverse sc: With right side facing, work sc from left to right *(Figs. 6a-d, page 47)*.

THROW

With **A**, ch 8; join with a slip st to form a ring.

Round 1: *Ch 4, 5 partial tr in ring, yo and pull through all 6 loops on hook—*cluster made*, ch 1 (top of cluster), ch 3 more, sc in ring; repeat from * 3 times more. Do not join.

Round 2: *12 Tr in top of next cluster, sc in next sc; repeat from * 3 times more; join with a slip st to first tr. Fasten off.

Round 3: With **B**, slip st in back loop of 9th tr *(Fig. 4, page 47)*; ch 4 (counts as first tr), partial BPtr in same st and next 3 tr, partial BPtr in next sc, partial BPtr in next 4 tr, yo and pull through all 10 loops on hook, ch 1 (top of cluster), ch 3 more; slip st through both loops at base of last BPtr made—*lower half of beginning circle made*.

Ch 4, partial BPtr in each of next 4 tr, yo and pull through all 5 loops on hook, ch 4, slip st through both loops at base of last BPtr made — *corner increase made*.

*Ch 4, partial BPtr in each of next (4 tr, sc, 4 tr), yo and pull through all 10 loops on hook, ch 4, slip st through both sts at base of last BPtr made—*lower half of circle made*, make corner increase; repeat from * 2 times more; join with a slip st to first ch of beginning ch-4.

▪Designed by Shari White.

Round 4: *8 Tr in center of lower half of circle of previous round, sc in next slip st, 12 tr in center st of corner increase, sc in next slip st; repeat from * 3 times more; join with a slip st to first tr—*upper half of circles made.* Fasten off.

Round 5: With **C**, slip st in back loop of 9th tr in last circle from previous round; make lower half of beginning circle then lower half of circle, make corner inc, *make lower half of circle 2 times, make corner increase; repeat from * 2 times more; join with a slip st to first ch of beginning ch-4.

Round 6: *[8 Tr in center of lower half of circle of previous round, sc in slip st] 2 times, 12 tr in center of corner increase, sc in slip st; repeat from * 3 times more; join with a slip st to first tr. Fasten off.

Continue in this manner to work 2 rounds of color **D**, then repeat color sequence of 2 rounds each of colors **A**, **B**, **C** and **D** until throw measures 50" x 50" (127 cm x 127 cm), ending with **A**. Fasten off.

Border

Round 1: With **B**, BPslip st in first tr of any corner circle; ch 3 (counts as dc), BPdc in next tr, *BPhdc in next 2 tr, BPsc in next 2 tr, ch 3, BPsc in next 2 tr, BPhdc in next 2 tr, BPdc in next 2 tr, [BPtr in sc, BPdc in next tr, BPhdc in next tr, BPsc in next 4 tr, BPhdc in next tr, BPdc in next tr] across to corner, BPtr in sc, BPdc in next 2 tr; repeat from * around, omitting last 2 BPdc; join with a slip st to top of beginning ch-3. Fasten off.

Round 2: Join **C** with a slip st in any corner ch-3 space; ch 1, *3 sc in ch-3 space, sc in each st across to corner; repeat from * around; join with a slip st to first sc. Fasten off.

Round 3: Join **D** with a slip st in any corner sc; ch 1, *3 sc in corner sc, sc in each sc across to corner; repeat from * around; join with a slip st to first sc. Fasten off.

Round 4: Join **A** with a slip st in any st; ch 1, reverse sc in each sc around; join with a slip st to first sc. Fasten off.

Circle Lapghan

(Shown on page 43)

◖■■☐◗ EASY

Lapghan measures 45" (114.5 cm) in diameter.

SHOPPING LIST

Yarn (Medium Weight)
RED HEART® Super Saver®:
- ☐ 0668 Honeydew **A** - 2 skeins
- ☐ 0320 Cornmeal **B** - 2 skeins
- ☐ 0406 Medium Thyme **C** - 2 skeins
- ☐ 0360 Café Latte **D** - 2 skeins

Crochet Hook
- ☐ 5.5 mm [US I-9]

Additional Supplies
- ☐ Yarn needle

GAUGE INFORMATION

Rounds 1-3 = 4" (10 cm) in diameter. **CHECK YOUR GAUGE.**
Use any size hook to obtain the gauge.

Stripe Sequence

Work 1 round with **A**,
2 rounds with **B**, 3 rounds with **C**,
2 rounds with **A**, 3 rounds with **D**,
2 rounds with **B**, 3 rounds with **C**,
3 rounds with **D**, 1 round with **A**,
2 rounds with **D**, 4 rounds with
B, 2 rounds with **D**, 4 rounds with
C, 2 rounds with **A**, 1 round with
B, 2 rounds with **D**, 3 rounds with
C, 3 rounds with **A**, 2 rounds with
B, 1 round with **D** and 1 round
with **A**.
Work these 47 rounds for
Stripe Sequence.

LAPGHAN

With **A**, ch 4; join with a slip st to
form a ring.

Round 1: Ch 4 (counts as dc and
ch 1), [dc in ring, ch 1] 11 times;
join with a slip st to 3rd ch of
beginning ch-4.

Fasten off.

Round 2: Join **B** with a slip st
in any ch-space; ch 3 (counts as
dc here and throughout), 2 dc
in same ch-space, [3 dc] in each
ch-space around; join with a slip st
to top of beginning ch-3.

Round 3: Ch 1, *sc in first dc of
dc-group, ch 3, skip next dc, sc
in next dc, FPtr around dc 2 rows
below *(Fig. 3)*; repeat from *
around; join with a slip st to
first sc.

Fasten off.

Fig. 3

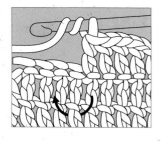

Follow Stripe Sequence to change
colors. If joining new color, join
in indicated st. If continuing with
same color, slip st to st indicated.

Round 4: In ch-space, ch 3 (counts
as dc here and throughout), 3 dc
in same ch-space, [4 dc] in each
ch-space around; join with a slip st
to top of beginning ch-3.

Round 5: In first dc of dc-group,
ch 1, *sc in first dc, ch 4, skip next
2 dc, sc in next dc, FPtr around
FPtr 2 rows below; repeat from *
around; join with a slip st to
first sc.

Round 6: In ch-space, ch 3, 4 dc in same ch-space, [5 dc] in each ch-space around; join with a slip st to top of beginning ch-3.

Round 7: In first dc of dc-group, ch 1, *sc in first sc, ch 5, skip next 3 dc, sc in next dc, FPtr around FPtr 2 rows below; repeat from * around; join with a slip st to first sc.

Round 8: In ch-space, ch 3, 5 dc in same ch-space, [6 dc] in each ch-space around; join with a slip st to top of beginning ch-3.

Round 9: In first dc of dc-group, ch 1, *sc in first dc, ch 6, skip next 4 dc, sc in next dc, FPtr around FPtr 2 rows below; repeat from * around; join with a slip st to first sc.

Round 10: In ch-space, ch 3, 6 dc in same ch-space, [7 dc] in each ch-space around; join with a slip st to top of beginning ch-3.

Round 11: In first dc of dc-group, ch 1, *sc in first dc, ch 1, skip next dc, sc in next dc, FPdc around next dc, sc in next dc, ch 1, skip next dc, sc in next dc, FPtr around FPtr 2 rows below; repeat from * around; join with a slip st to first sc.

Round 12: In ch-space, ch 3, 2 dc in same ch-space, [3 dc] in each ch-space around; join with a slip st to top of beginning ch-3.

Round 13: In first dc of dc-group, ch 1, *sc in first dc, ch 3, skip next dc, sc in next dc, FPtr around post st 2 rows below; repeat from * around; join with a slip st to first sc.

Keeping in Stripe Sequence, repeat Rounds 4-13, 3 times more.

Repeat Rounds 12-13 once.

Repeat Rounds 4-5 once.

Fasten off.

Weave in ends.

General Instructions

ABBREVIATIONS

BP	Back Post	dec	decrease
BPdc	Back Post double crochet(s)	FPtr	Front Post treble crochet(s)
BPhdc	Back Post half double crochet(s)	hdc	half double crochet(s)
BPsc	Back Post single crochet(s)	inc	increase
		MC	Main Color
		mm	millimeters
BPtr	Back Post treble crochet(s)	sc	single crochet(s)
		sc3tog	single crochet 3 together
ch(s)	chain(s)	st(s)	stitch(es)
cm	centimeters	tog	together
dc	double crochet(s)	tr	treble crochet(s)
dc2tog	double crochet 2 together	yo	yarn over

SYMBOLS & TERMS

*, ** or *** — repeat whatever follows the *, ** or *** as indicated.

( ) or [ ] — work directions in parentheses or brackets the number of times specified.

GAUGE

Gauge refers to the number of stitches and rows in a given area. When making projects, ensure that your project is the correct finished size and is to gauge. Working the area as stated in the pattern and then measure to check that it agrees with the gauge given. If it is not the same size, change your hook size. If it is too large, use a smaller hook. If it is too small, use a larger hook size.

CROCHET TERMINOLOGY

UNITED STATES		INTERNATIONAL
slip stitch (slip st)	=	single crochet (sc)
single crochet (sc)	=	double crochet (dc)
half double crochet (hdc)	=	half treble crochet (htr)
double crochet (dc)	=	treble crochet(tr)
treble crochet (tr)	=	double treble crochet (dtr)
double treble crochet (dtr)	=	triple treble crochet (ttr)
triple treble crochet (tr tr)	=	quadruple treble crochet (qtr)
skip	=	miss

Yarn Weight Symbol & Names	LACE 0	SUPER FINE 1	FINE 2	LIGHT 3	MEDIUM 4	BULKY 5	SUPER BULKY 6
Type of Yarns in Category	Fingering, 10-count crochet thread	Sock, Fingering Baby	Sport, Baby	DK, Light Worsted	Worsted, Afghan, Aran	Chunky, Craft, Rug	Bulky, Roving
Crochet Gauge* Ranges in Single Crochet to 4" (10 cm)	32-42 double crochets**	21-32 sts	16-20 sts	12-17 sts	11-14 sts	8-11 sts	5-9 sts
Advised Hook Size Range	Steel*** 6,7,8 Regular hook B-1	B-1 to E-4	E-4 to 7	7 to I-9	I-9 to K-10.5	K-10.5 to M-13	M-13 and larger

*GUIDELINES ONLY: The chart above reflects the most commonly used gauges and hook sizes for specific yarn categories.

** Lace weight yarns are usually crocheted on larger-size hooks to create lacy openwork patterns. Accordingly, a gauge range is difficult to determine. Always follow the gauge stated in your pattern.

*** Steel crochet hooks are sized differently from regular hooks–the higher the number the smaller the hook, which is the reverse of regular hook sizing.

■☐☐☐☐ BEGINNER	Projects for first-time crocheters using basic stitches. Minimal shaping.
■■☐☐☐ EASY	Projects using yarn with basic stitches, repetitive stitch patterns, simple color changes, and simple shaping and finishing.
■■■☐☐ INTERMEDIATE	Projects using a variety of techniques, such as basic lace patterns or color patterns, mid-level shaping and finishing.
■■■■☐ EXPERIENCED	Projects with intricate stitch patterns, techniques and dimension, such as non-repeating patterns, multi-color techniques, fine threads, small hooks, detailed shaping and refined finishing.

CROCHET HOOKS														
U.S.	B-1	C-2	D-3	E-4	F-5	G-6	H-8	I-9	J-10	K-10½	L-11	M/N-13	N/P-15	P/Q	Q	S
Metric - mm	2.25	2.75	3.25	3.5	3.75	4	5	5.5	6	6.5	8	9	10	15	16	19

BACK LOOPS ONLY

Work only in loop(s) indicated by arrow *(Fig. 4)*.

Fig. 4

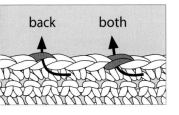

POST STITCH

Work around the post of the stitch indicated, inserting the hook in direction of the arrow *(Fig. 5)*.

Fig. 5

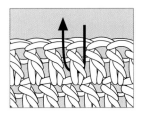

REVERSE SINGLE CROCHET

Working from **left** to **right**, *insert hook in st to right of hook *(Fig. 6a)*, yo and draw through, under and to the left of loop on hook (2 loops on hook) *(Fig. 6b)*, yo and draw through both loops on hook *(Fig. 6c)* (**reverse sc made**, *Fig. 6d*); repeat from * around.

Fig. 6a

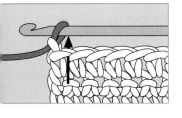

Fig. 6b

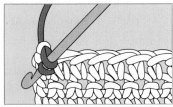

Fig. 6c

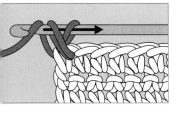

Fig. 6d

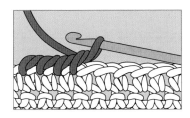

Yarn Information

The projects in this book were created with **RED HEART®** yarns. For best results, we recommend following the pattern exactly as written. Be sure to purchase the amounts recommended in the pattern, and retain your labels. Always follow the care instructions provided on the label.

RED HEART® Super Saver® Art. E300 available in solid colors 7 oz (198 g), 364 yd (333 m); multi colors, flecks and prints 5 oz (141 g), 244 yd (223 m) skeins.

RED HEART® With Love®, Art. E400 available in solid colors 7 oz (198 g), 370 yd (338 m) multi colors 5 oz (141 g), 230 yd (211 m) skeins.

RED HEART® Super Saver® Chunky™, Art. E778, available in solid colors 6 oz (170 g), 207 yd (189 m) skeins.

For more ideas and inspiration -

www.redheart.com   www.facebook.com/redheartyarns
www.pinterest.com/redheartyarns   www.twitter.com/redheartyarns
www.youtube.com/redheartyarns   Instagram @redheartyarns

We have made every effort to ensure that these instructions are accurate and complete. We cannot, however, be responsible for human error, typographical mistakes, or variations in individual work.

Copyright © 2014 by Leisure Arts, Inc., 104 Champs Blvd., STE 100, Maumelle, AR 72113-6738, www.leisurearts.com. All rights reserved. This publication is protected under federal copyright laws. Reproduction or distribution of this publication or any other Leisure Arts publication, including publications which are out of print, is prohibited unless specifically authorized. This includes, but is not limited to, any form of reproduction or distribution on or through the Internet, including posting, scanning, or e-mail transmission.

© 2014 Coats & Clark, all rights reserved.